Who will be my Father?

The true story of
Wilson Bugembe

Written by Cheri Bowling

Illustrated by Kymber Janes

*"My story would be a sad one without Christ;
with Christ it is a story of HOPE."*
Wilson Bugembe

*"See how great a love the Father has bestowed upon us,
that we should be called children of God; and such we are."*
1 John 3:1

Wilson sat outside the door of his home in the Ugandan village of Masaka. His eyes were fixed on the road that led away from the small bungalow where he lived with his father and four brothers.

Although his mother had recently died of AIDS, an illness that took the lives of many in his country, Wilson couldn't believe she was never coming home.

Day after day he sat and watched and waited.

"One day I'm going to see her," thought Wilson. But with each passer-by that wasn't his mother, Wilson's hopes began to fade.

Wilson's dad missed his wife terribly, but it broke his heart to see Wilson waiting for something that would never happen. "Wilson, your mom isn't going to come home," he said as he pulled him into his arms and held him tightly. "You have to learn to live without her," he whispered.

Wilson thought his heart would burst with sadness as he wept against his father's chest.

Several months passed, and then Wilson's dad become ill. When he was taken from the local clinic to the hospital, Wilson feared that the nightmare they had been living since his mother's death was going to take an even more frightening turn. "This is exactly what happened to Mom," he thought as he tried to calm the fear rising up within him.

Wilson and his brothers were sent to stay with their grandmother.

One day his grandmother called them all together and said, "Wilson, your father has returned home and has asked to see you and your brothers."

So the five boys began the five mile trip from their grandmother's house to their home. On the way Wilson wrestled with his fears. "It's happening all over again! How can this be possible?" he wondered. "Mom asked to see us when she knew she was going to die."

The thought of his father dying was more than Wilson could bear.

Wilson's father summoned his children to his bedside, then dismissed all but one—Wilson. "Come closer, Wilson," he whispered. Wilson moved close to the bed where his dad lay. "I have AIDS," he said softly. "I am going to die. Please be the father and mother to your brothers. Three of your brothers are sick with HIV, the virus that causes AIDS, but you and one other do not have it. I don't want to tell you which, because I want you to love them all equally. For now, they will all go to different relatives, but when you grow up, I want you to bring the family together again."

As Wilson's dad lay dying, many people came to pray for him. He had many friends of many different faiths who all came to pray.

One day a pastor came to pray for him. When he prayed, he asked for Wilson's dad to accept Jesus as his Savior. Wilson's dad died soon after he left. Wilson was devastated.

Wilson was also very angry with the pastor!

In fact, Wilson was so angry that he made a very serious decision. "I will never, never give my life to Jesus!" he declared.

It was a very sad day when Wilson and his brothers went to live with different members of their family.

Although Wilson's family loved him, there were a lot of people living with them and a lot of chores to do. Wilson was so sad that he had a very hard time fitting into his new surroundings.

One day Wilson decided it would be better for him to be on his own, so he ran away and began to live on the streets of Kampala. It wasn't long before Wilson found himself eating out of garbage cans and begging for food. At night, he slept under a mango tree on a busy city street.

It was a hard life.

Wilson dreamed of the day when he could fulfill his promise to his father to take care of his brothers.

Desperate to find a way to finish his education, Wilson decided to seek help at a nearby church. Although he still didn't like pastors, Wilson considered it his only option. Mustering up courage, he crossed the street and entered the church office. "I'm here to talk with the pastor," Wilson explained to the young woman who looked up as he entered the room. "He's not here but should return shortly," she said. "Why don't you wait for him? What is your name?"

"Wilson," he said slowly, realizing he had almost forgotten his own name! On the street he was known simply as "Yellow" because of the yellow shirt he always wore.

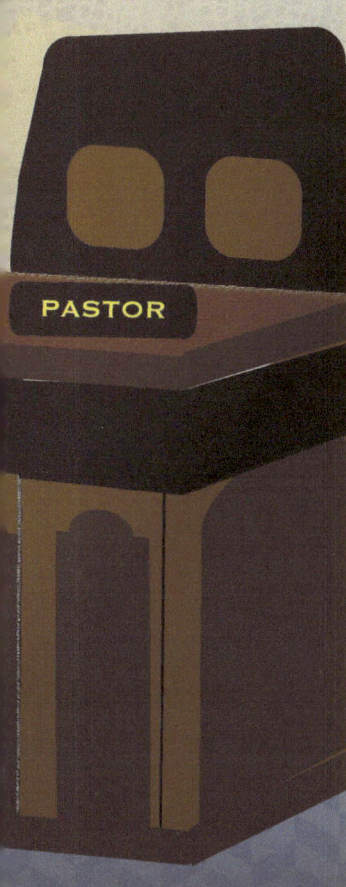

Soon the pastor returned, but instead of greeting Wilson, he began to complain, "Who allowed this dirty boy to sit in my seats?"

As a sign of honor, Wilson fell at the man's feet. "Please, can you help me?" Wilson pleaded. "My parents have died, and I need to go back to school so that I can take care of my family."

"I don't talk to street kids. I don't talk to dirty boys," the pastor barked. "Get out of here!"

Stunned and disappointed, Wilson stood and ran from the office.

Desperate thoughts ran wildly through his mind. "Life on the street was no life. There is no hope without an education. I just want to go to heaven and be with my mom and dad!"

Wilson cried as he ran through the traffic on the busy street in front of the pastor's office. Cars honked horns and swerved to miss him as he purposely tried to be hit by the cars and trucks pulsing through the street.

Blinded by the tears pouring from his eyes, Wilson suddenly found himself pulled from the traffic and engulfed in a huge hug.

Thoughts of his father's hugs quickly flooded his mind.

Looking up, Wilson found himself staring into the eyes of a man whom he had often seen walking along the street. His name was Patrick.

"What are you doing?" Patrick asked. "Do you want to kill yourself?"

"I have to go back to school," Wilson cried out through his tears. Looking down at Wilson, Patrick was filled with compassion. There was something special about him. "I am very poor," said Patrick, "but I can take you to a place where you might be able to find the help you need."

Patrick's hug saved Wilson's life that day.

Patrick took Wilson to church with him. On the second Sunday he attended, Wilson was asked to tell his story. When he finished he was asked if he wanted to give his life to Jesus. "No," said Wilson. "I just want to go back to school so I can have a future and get my brothers back together."

"Is there anyone here who would be a father to Wilson and see that he gets an education," the pastor asked the congregation. Wilson waited as the church became very quiet. After what seemed a very long time, a man raised his hand. His name was Stephan.

"Wilson will be my son. I will take him from today on," Stephan said. It just so happened that Stephan was the director of a school. It was a good school called Highway College.

Suddenly, Wilson's life changed. For the first time in a very long time, he had a bed and bed covers all his own. He was very happy.

But Wilson's happiness didn't last long. Feeling like he didn't fit in, he soon became a loner. He had no friends and hardly ever spoke to anyone. Teachers felt sorry for him and treated him differently than other students, rarely punishing him for poor performance or wrong behavior.

And, while his fellow classmates often had visitors, Wilson had no family or friends come to see him.

All of these things made Wilson feel very alone.

One day Stephan came to see Wilson and asked for a favor.

"Wilson, I hate to see you alone all the time. Would you go to the Christian Fellowship that meets to pray, sing and study the Bible?"

Out of respect and gratitude for all Stephan was doing for him, Wilson agreed to go, but although his body was there, his heart was not.

Then he met Diane.

Diane was beautiful and Wilson decided to win her heart. "Will you be my girlfriend?" Wilson asked one evening when they were alone together.

"Aren't you the boy from the street?" she asked.

Wilson suddenly realized that everyone knew he was different from them! He blushed with embarrassment.

Then Diane smiled at him and said sweetly, "Keep coming to fellowship, and we'll see if I love you."

So Wilson continued to attend the fellowship and began playing the African drums with their choir. He quickly discovered that he had a natural musical talent.

After playing with the group for a while, Wilson realized that the fellowship choir needed someone to help organize them.

"Can I help you?" Wilson asked Jolie, the music director. "Of course!" she responded.

The next time the fellowship met, everyone was very pleased with the music. "Wilson, you must stay and continue to help us!" exclaimed Jolie.

Wilson was glad. It felt good to belong.

Wilson knew he was only at fellowship for Stephan, Diane, and now the music, but his heart was still closed to Jesus.

Then one day, in the middle of worship, Wilson realized God loved him. Suddenly, he found himself on his face, crying his eyes out and confessing, "God, I'm so sorry. I know you love me. I know you love me."

From that moment on, Wilson's life was never the same.

Three fellow students came to faith in Jesus around the same time as Wilson—Philip, Wilfred and Ben. Although they knew little about sharing their new faith, the group was determined to bring all the students at Highway College who didn't know Jesus to faith in their Savior. However, many did not like their message, and much turmoil came from their efforts.

To calm things down, the headmaster closed down the fellowship. But Wilson and his friends wouldn't be stopped. They placed notes around the school that said, "Nobody can stop what the Lord has started. Open the fellowship soon!"

Then the Spirit of God began to move, and revival broke out at the school. It wasn't long before the fellowship was allowed to meet again.

One day Wilson and his friends were called to the headmaster's office. "What have we done wrong?" they wondered as they headed to his office.

When they arrived, they discovered the mother of one of the students had come to thank them for the healing of her child. "During your fellowship, my child was healed from a tumor," she said with tears in her eyes. Wilson and his friends rejoiced!

Revival continued at the school and more students were healed. More parents came to thank them for praying for their children. It wasn't long before the revival spread to the surrounding schools. It was a very exciting time!

As Wilson's graduation drew near, the headmaster called Wilson into his office once again. "Wilson," he asked, "before you leave, would you write a song about your experiences these past few years at the school?"

So Wilson wrote a song. He called it "Yellow." It was about how God had blessed him, taking him from being a street boy with one yellow shirt and no hope for the future, to a beloved child of the King. The headmaster was so impressed with the song, he asked Wilson to participate in a talent show that was coming to town. A few weeks later, Wilson sang "Yellow" at the talent show.

"I want to announce the winner and the song that has touched everyone," declared the show's director. Not wanting to miss seeing the winner revealed, Wilson stood up. "It is Wilson Bugembe and the song is 'Yellow!'" Wilson was so shocked to hear his name that he burst into tears.

From that day on, when Wilson walked the streets of Kampala, the children would call to him, "Hey, Wilson! We saw you on TV! Is it true you used to live on the street, too?"

Because all the children on the street reminded Wilson of his brothers, he was determined to help them. Wilson decided he would use the winnings from the talent show to provide a home for as many children as he could.

So Wilson rented a one room apartment with no window and only one bed. Then one by one Wilson brought street kids into his new home to live. In a very short time there were nine kids living with him and his friends, Wilfred, Ben and Phillip, in his tiny apartment with only one bed.

Every Sunday, Wilson and his friends would walk with the children to a nearby church. "Hey, let's start our own fellowship," someone said one Sunday as they made the trip to the service. And so they did.

They named the church, Light the World Church. It was the kid's church, and it met under a mango tree in the valley. With God's blessing, it grew and grew. In just a few short years, the church grew from 9 to 5000!

Wilson continues to write songs and sing them around the world. He has sung before presidents and princes. But, rather than using his talent to become rich and famous, Wilson sings for the children.

"The Lord God has been good to me," said Wilson. "He has turned every disappointment into an appointment. I am not so sad about my Dad and Mom dying anymore. Although they had plans for me, the Lord had His own plan, and His plan was the best. Jeremiah 29:11 says, 'I know the plans I have for you,' declares the Lord, 'to give you a future and a hope.'

"My story would be a sad one without Christ; with Christ it is a story of HOPE."

Currently, Wilson is the lead pastor and founder of Light the World Church, a church of about 5000 and growing. He is one of the directors of Mercy Childcare where over 160 children live. He is the vision bearer of Worship Night, an event that attracts between 40,000 and 50,000 believers from all over the world to worship the living God.

If you wish to learn more about Wilson's ministry, you can do so through the U.S. nonprofit organization Equipping Network at dennis.enetwork@gmail.org.

I call Him Daddy

"I dedicate this song to all orphans all over the world. Jesus is the father to the fatherless. I was a street kid eating from the garbage, shedding tears for my parents but Jesus loved me. I stand to testify that He is the father to the fatherless and mother to the motherless. Don't give up. Try Jesus. He loves you." Wilson Bugembe

My Jesus is known by many names.
Everyone has got a name they call him.
For some he is a son of Mary,
to some he is a Jewish carpenter,
to some he is a giver of bread.
My Jesus is known by many names.

My Master is known by many names.
Every one has got a name they call him.
To some he is a son of Mary,
and to some he is a giver of bread.
To some he is a little son of Joseph.
My Jesus is known by many names.

But for me, I call him Daddy.
He's been my daddy when I had no daddy.
He's been my mama when I had no mother.

I call him Daddy. Yes, he is.
Yes, he is.

Chorus
He is the father to the fatherless
and the mother to the motherless.
He is full of love, in season and out of season.
I call him Daddy.
Yes, he is.

You loved me when I had no lover.
You clothed me when I was naked.
Oh, you were my food when I had nothing to eat.
I call you Daddy.
Yes, you are.

The link to the MP3 version of the song I call Him Daddy - www.hipipo.com/radio/28/Pastor-Wilson-Bugembe/Wilson-Bugembe-I-Call-Him-Daddy

www.ingramcontent.com/pod-product-compliance
Lightning Source LLC
LaVergne TN
LVHW072117070426
835510LV00003B/104